A TRUE BOOK™

# The Spanish Missions of California

MEGAN GENDELL

Children's Press®
An imprint of Scholastic Inc.

New York   Toronto   London   Auckland   Sydney
Mexico City   New Delhi   Hong Kong

**Content Consultant**
Kristina W. Foss
Museum Director, Santa Barbara Mission Museum

Library of Congress Cataloging-in-Publication Data

Gendell, Megan.
  Spanish missions of California / by Megan Gendell.
      p. cm.—(A true book)
  Includes bibliographical references and index.
  ISBN-13: 978-0-531-20577-8 (lib. bdg.)      978-0-531-21240-0 (pbk.)
  ISBN-10: 0-531-20577-0 (lib. bdg.)      0-531-21240-8 (pbk.)

  1. California—History—To 1846—Juvenile literature. 2. Missions, Spanish—California—History—Juvenile literature. 3. Indians of North America—Missions—California—Juvenile literature. 4. Franciscans—Missions—California—History—Juvenile literature. I. Title. II. Series.

  F864.G384 2010
  979.4'02—dc22                                      2009014238

All rights reserved. Published in 2010 by Children's Press, an imprint of Scholastic Inc.
Published simultaneously in Canada. Printed in China.
SCHOLASTIC, CHILDREN'S PRESS, A TRUE BOOK, and associated logos are trademarks and/or registered trademarks of Scholastic Inc.

2 3 4 5 6 7 8 9 10 R 19 18 17 16 15 14 13 12 11 10                    62

# Find the Truth!

**Everything** you are about to read is true *except* for one of the sentences on this page.

Which one is **TRUE**?

**T or F**  There were no oranges in California before the missionaries brought them.

**T or F**  A person could walk from one California mission to the next in an hour.

Find the answers in this book.

# Contents

Mission San Gabriel

4

The bells at Mission San Gabriel Arcángel could be heard 10 miles away.

## THE **BIG** TRUTH!

## El Camino Real

## 5 The End of the Missions

Father Serra

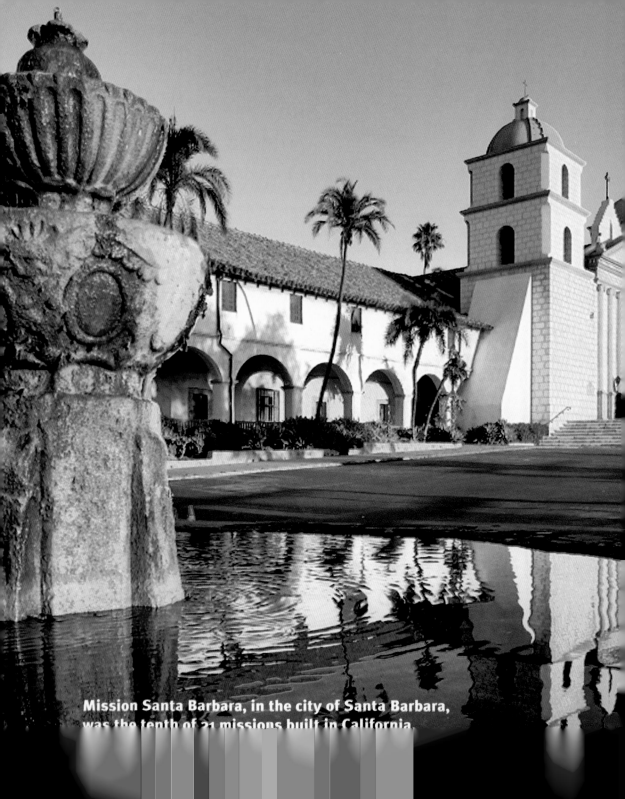

Mission Santa Barbara, in the city of Santa Barbara, was the tenth of 21 missions built in California.

# CHAPTER 1

# Europeans Arrive

In 1769, priests from Spain began founding missions in California. These priests, or **padres** (PAH-drayz), were the first Europeans to settle in California. The missions they founded were like small villages where they tried to **convert** Native Americans to Christianity.

 Most California missions are still active churches.

# Claiming North America

Before building missions in California, the Spanish had taken over other regions of North America. In the 1500s, they conquered what is now Mexico.

To the north of Mexico was the land that is now the United States. By the mid-1700s, Spain had founded missions in what are today the states of New Mexico, Texas, Arizona, and Florida. The Spanish moved on to California next because they wanted to claim that land before any other European nation did.

By the 1820s, 21 missions were built along the coast of California.

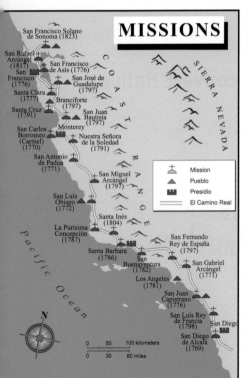

**MISSIONS**

San Francisco Solano de Sonoma (1823)
San Rafael Arcángel (1817)
San Francisco de Asís (1776)
San Francisco (1776)
San José de Guadalupe (1797)
Santa Clara (1777)
Branciforte (1797)
Santa Cruz (1791)
San Juan Bautista (1797)
San Carlos Borromeo (Carmel) (1770)
Monterey
Nuestra Señora de la Soledad (1791)
San Antonio de Padua (1771)
San Miguel Arcángel (1797)
San Luis Obispo (1772)
Santa Inés (1804)
La Purísima Concepción (1787)
Santa Barbara (1786)
San Buenaventura (1782)
San Fernando Rey de España (1797)
San Gabriel Arcángel (1771)
Los Angeles (1781)
San Juan Capistrano (1776)
San Luis Rey de Francia (1798)
San Diego
San Diego de Alcalá (1769)

COAST RANGE
SIERRA NEVADA
Pacific Ocean

✝ Mission
▲ Pueblo
🏰 Presidio
═══ El Camino Real

0   50   100 kilometers
0   30   60 miles

**This map shows all of the missions built in California.**

8

Some Native Americans learned Spanish so they could work with the missionaries.

## Men with a Mission

When the padres arrived in California, they met many Native American groups, including the Chumash (SHOO-mash), Salinans (suh-LEE-nunz), and Costanoans (kos-tuh-NOH-unz). The padres lived at the missions and dedicated themselves to making these groups more like Spanish people. The padres introduced Native Americans to Spanish food, clothing, and architecture (ar-kuh-TEK-chur).

Spanish priests and soldiers explore the land that later became San Diego.

# CHAPTER 2

# Settling the Land

The padres chose the locations of their missions carefully. The first missions in California were built near bays so ships could reach them with supplies. Many of California's major cities formed around these original mission sites. The padres also chose spots near rivers so they would have water for the crops grown on mission farmland.

Some California cities were named after missions, including San Diego and San Francisco.

# Getting Started

When starting a mission, the padres first constructed simple shelters from tree branches. This gave them a place to live and conduct **mass**. Later, the padres would put up actual buildings. The Native Americans who had always used this land for living, farming, and hunting were forced to fight to protect it from being taken over. To defend themselves, the Spanish built **presidios** (prih-SEE-dee-ohz), or forts, near a few missions. Soldiers at the presidios guarded the missions and the California coastline.

Native Americans and Spanish soldiers gather around as a padre conducts mass.

It could take several years to build a mission church.

## Moving In

The Native Americans in California were not used to outsiders. To show they were friendly, the padres offered the Native people food and clothing.

Native Americans who lived at missions had to get used to a new way of life. They were forced to follow strict schedules of work, prayers, and lessons. They also had to help the padres build and care for the missions' property. Children had to obey the padres as well as their parents.

# Hard Times

Mission living was filled with challenges. It took time for the missions' farms to begin producing crops. Until then, the padres relied on supply ships from Spain to bring food. Sometimes these ships were delayed or got lost.

The weather also caused problems. When there wasn't enough rain, **droughts** (DROWTS) sometimes killed crops. Too much rain caused rivers to flood, and the water destroyed mission buildings. Buildings were also ruined by earthquakes.

Spanish ships carried supplies to the missions.

# Father of the Missions

The best-known padre in California was Father Junípero Serra (hoo-NIP-eh-roh SEH-rah). As a young priest in Spain, Father Serra dreamed of becoming a missionary. His dream finally came true when he arrived in California in 1769. Father Serra's goal was to create a chain of missions along the coast that would serve all of the Native Americans in California. By the time of his death in 1784, he had founded nine of California's 21 missions.

**Father Serra believed that he was giving Native Americans a better life.**

Like all California missions,
Mission San Gabriel included
many different buildings.

16

# CHAPTER 3

# Mission Life

Typically, two padres and a few soldiers lived at a mission. They were joined by many Native Americans. The padres taught the Native Americans about Christianity. Then they **baptized** them, sprinkling holy water over them in a Christian ceremony. Native Americans who had been recently baptized were called **neophytes** (NEE-uh-fites). Neophytes were required to live at the mission, where they would work and learn.

Neophytes were usually allowed only short visits away from the missions.

# Spreading Religion

Native Americans who did not live at the missions still visited them for food and water. This was especially true during a drought in the early 1800s. The missions also attracted Native Americans who were curious about Christianity.

The missionaries used paintings and music to encourage Native people to accept Christianity.

Many missionaries learned the languages that the Native Americans spoke and preached to them in those languages.

18

# Traditional Beliefs

Even though many Native Americans joined in daily prayers at the missions, they still had their own beliefs and traditions that they did not want to give up. Many continued to honor the spirits they had always believed in. The padres could urge Native Americans to say Christian prayers and sing Christian hymns (HIMS), but they couldn't force them to change their beliefs. After having the Spanish force their ways upon them, many Native Americans lost their ancient languages and **cultures**.

**This picture shows Christian padres baptizing a Native American child.**

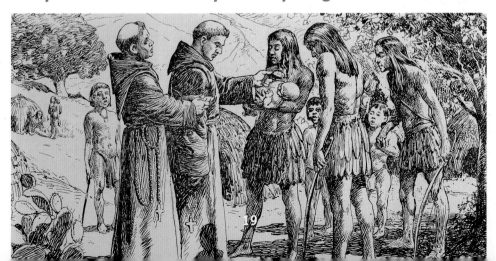

Wheat was one of the major crops grown at California missions.

## All in a Day's Work

Neophyte men and women were given daily assignments. This included making **adobe** (uh-DOE-bee) bricks and roof tiles for mission buildings. They also raised cows and sheep and planted and harvested crops for the missions' food supply. Some Native people learned to make candles, rope, or shoes. Women cooked, weaved, and washed clothes. The items that the Native Americans made were sold to help the missions.

# Mission Bells

Bells were hung at missions throughout California, and padres rang them for different purposes. The bells informed Native Americans that a new mission had been started out in the wilderness. They also alerted people that it was time to gather for prayers. Different bell tones indicated whether it was time to eat or pray. Bells were also rung to celebrate weddings, religious holidays, and other events.

Mission San Gabriel Arcángel (ark-AN-hel), in the town of San Gabriel, had six bells. The largest weighed more than 1 ton (0.9 metric tons).

# Mission Meals

The padres brought seeds and animals with them from Spain to California. This allowed them to have foods from home. People living at missions ate beef, beans, and vegetables. They also ground corn to make bread, and cooked corn to make soup. Native Americans sometimes left the missions to gather the wild nuts, seeds, and fruits they were used to eating.

Thousands of meals were prepared in mission kitchens every day.

This kitchen at **Mission San Carlos Borromeo de Carmelo** has been restored to look as it would have more than 200 years ago.

# Grown in California

Today, much of the United States's orange, lemon, and grapefruit crops come from California. But before the Spanish missions, no citrus fruit grew in the state. With orange seeds they brought from Spain, the padres planted California's first orange grove in 1804 at Mission San Gabriel Arcángel. In 1841, a man named William Wolfskill used trees from San Gabriel to start a business growing oranges. By the late 1800s, California oranges were being shipped all over the country.

Native Americans and padres raised sheep, horses, and other animals at the missions.

# From Sheep to Cloth

Sheep were raised on the missions' farms to provide wool for clothing. The padres taught neophyte men to herd the sheep and to shear their wool. They showed neophyte women how to wash the wool and spin it into yarn. The women also learned to weave fabric on large **looms**. From this fabric, they made clothing and blankets.

# Holidays

Life at the missions was not all work. The missions celebrated about 90 holidays each year. These included Christian holidays such as Christmas and Easter. Each mission also held a feast honoring the saint it was named after. Events such as weddings were celebrated like holidays. On these days, nobody at the mission worked. Instead, they held parades, danced, and sang religious songs.

On holidays, the padres wore special robes made with gold and silver threads.

**This robe was worn by Father Serra.**

Mission San Carlos Borromeo de
Carmelo in the town of Carmel, California

# CHAPTER 4

# Many Missions

Each of the California missions had something that made it special, but they all had the same basic design. A mission included a church, workshops, and living spaces for the padres and Native Americans. The buildings were usually arranged in a square. In the center was a courtyard with gardens and a fountain. Usually the **facades** (fuh-SAHDZ) were curved and had arches.

San Carlos Borromeo de Carmelo was the first California mission built of stone.

# Mission San Luis Rey de Francia

Mission San Luis Rey de Francia (frawn-SEE-uh), in Oceanside, California, is nicknamed "King of the Missions" because it was the largest. In 1832, San Luis Rey was home to 2,788 neophytes. Corn, wheat, grapes, peppers, and many other crops were grown at the mission. Its farmland produced so much food that some was sent to other missions. With its lovely gardens, many people today consider it the most beautiful mission in California.

**The first pepper tree ever grown in California was in San Luis Rey's gardens.**

## Mission La Purisíma Concepción

After earthquakes and heavy rains destroyed Mission La Purisíma Concepción (poo-ree-SEE-mah kone-sep-see-OWN), it was rebuilt several miles away. Today, it is a museum where visitors can tour a pottery workshop and a weaving room once used by neophytes. Other rooms and the chapel still look much as they would have 200 years ago.

**Mission San Juan Bautista is in the city of San Juan Bautista.**

## Mission San Juan Bautista

Mission San Juan Bautista (bau-TEE-stah) was nicknamed the "Mission of Music." It earned this nickname because a choir of Native American boys performed for its visitors.

At San Juan Bautista and many other missions, covered passageways called **arcades** connected different buildings. They also kept missions cool in the summer and dry during rain.

# Mission San José

Music was also important at Mission San José, in the city of Fremont, where 30 Native American musicians played in a band. Father Narciso (nar-SEE-soh) Duran worked at the mission for 27 years and taught the band members to play instruments, including flutes and violins.

People came from all over California to listen to Mission San José's band.

# Mission San Juan Capistrano

Within Mission San Juan Capistrano (kap-ih-STRAH-noh) is Serra's Chapel, where Father Serra was said to have led mass. It is the oldest building in California still in use. A bottle baked inside one of its adobe bricks contains a description of the mission's founding.

In 1812, an earthquake destroyed a huge stone church at this mission. The church remains in ruins today. This mission is famous for swallows, a type of bird that nests in the ruins. The swallows fly south each October and return to Capistrano each March.

Mission San Juan Capistrano, in San Juan Capistrano, is called the "Jewel of the California missions."

**Salinan Indians painted colorful murals on the walls of Mission San Miguel Arcángel in the 1820s.**

## Mission San Miguel Arcángel

Mission buildings were usually plain white on the outside. The walls inside were often beautifully decorated. Inside Mission San Miguel Arcángel, in the town of San Miguel, neophytes painted the walls to look like wallpaper and wood.

## missions on El Camino Real

- San Francisco de Solano
- San Rafael Arcángel
- San Francisco de Asís
- San José
- Santa Clara de Asís
- Santa Cruz
- San Juan Bautista
- San Carlos Borromeo de Carmelo
- Nuestra Señora de la Soledad
- San Antonio de Padua
- La Purísima Concepción
- San Miguel Arcángel
- San Luis Obispo de Tolosa
- Santa Inés
- San Buenaventura
- Santa Bárbara
- San Fernando Rey de España
- San Gabriel Arcángel
- San Juan Capistrano
- San Diego de Alcalá
- San Luis Rey de Francia

▲ When Father Serra founded Mission San Antonio de Padua (PAH-joo-wuh), he hung a bell from the branch of an oak tree. Today, that bell still hangs in one of San Antonio's bell towers.

▼ Stories about gold hidden by the padres caused people to dig up the church floor and walls after San Fernando Rey de España (es-PAH-nyah) was abandoned.

# El Camino Real

A path called El Camino Real (EL kuh-MEE-noh ray-UL), which means "the King's Highway," or "the Royal Road," connected the missions. Over time, the padres built so many missions along El Camino Real that a person could walk from one to the next in just a few days.

▲ Mission San Rafael Arcángel included a successful farm. Many horses, sheep, and cattle were raised there. San Rafael was especially well known for its pears.

A padre and Native Americans pray at a mission.

# CHAPTER 5

# The End of the Missions

The padres punished the Native Americans if they did not follow Christian rules. Neophytes could be whipped or locked up if they skipped mass or work. In 1775, Native people at Mission San Diego de Alcalá fought back against the padres' cruel treatment. The mission padres left and didn't return for a year.

By 1833, about 31,000 Christian Native Americans lived near the California missions.

# Spanish Diseases

Disease spread easily in missions because people lived crowded together. At the California missions, Native Americans were exposed to diseases brought by Europeans. These diseases had long existed in Europe, so people there could live with them. But the diseases were new and deadly for Native Americans, and their communities were devastated by them.

**Crosses and stones mark graves at the mission in Carmel, California.**

# Timeline of the California Missions

## 1769

**Father Serra founds Mission San Diego de Alcalá, California's first mission.**

## 1812

**Earthquakes damage several missions.**

# The End of an Era

As of 1821, Mexico was no longer ruled by Spain. So in 1833, Mexico **secularized** (SEK-yuh-luh-rized) the missions, taking them out of the church's control. The mission land was divided up. Most of it was sold to Mexican ranchers. Native Americans ended up moving away from the missions.

These mission buildings north of Los Angeles were abandoned after Mexico secularized the missions.

## 1823

**Mission San Francisco de Solano is founded in the town of Sonoma. It is the last mission established in California.**

## 1833

**Mexico orders that the California missions can no longer be religious places.**

39

# Rebuilding and Restoring

Once people moved away from the missions, the buildings were no longer cared for. Many fell into ruins. Since the late 1800s, many missions have been restored. The buildings are being strengthened for protection from earthquakes. At some missions, such as La Purisíma, copies of the original buildings have been built.

**A colorful doorway welcomes visitors to Mission La Purisíma.**

Father Junípero Serra is buried at Mission San Carlos Borromeo de Carmelo.

## Missions Today

The buildings that are still standing at the missions are some of the oldest structures in California. Visitors from all over the world attend mass in their chapels. They are able to view clothing, bells, and other items the padres used. They also tour the grounds and beautiful gardens.

**Luiseno (loo-ee-SAY-no) Indians hold a ceremony at Mission San Luis Rey every year.**

# Traces of the Past

Today, some Native Americans continue to worship at California missions. For example, a chapel run by Mission San Luis Rey serves Native Americans from the Pala Reservation.

Mission San Luis Rey and California's 20 other missions are an important part of the state's history. To make sure they are protected, the California Missions Foundation was set up to repair the missions and their artwork. ★

# True Statistics

**Number of California missions:** 21

**First mission:** Mission San Diego de Alcalá, founded by Father Serra in 1769

**Last mission:** Mission San Francisco de Solano, founded by Father José de Altimíra in 1823

**Largest mission:** San Luis Rey, with 2,788 neophytes in 1832

**Length of the California Mission Trail:** About 600 mi. (1,000 km)

**Plants the padres brought to California:** Oranges, grapes, peppers, corn, oats, wheat, beans, and many more

**Animals the padres brought to California:** cows, mules, horses, pigs, sheep, goats, and more

Pepper tree

## Did you find the truth?

**T** There were no oranges in California before the missionaries brought them.

**F** A person could walk from one California mission to the next in an hour.

# Resources

## Books

Bial, Raymond. *Missions and Presidios.* New York: Children's Press, 2004.

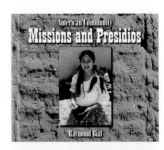

Bowler, Sarah. *Father Junípero Serra and the California Missions.* Chanhassen, MN: Child's World, 2003.

Ditchfield, Christin. *Spanish Missions.* New York: Children's Press, 2006.

Heinrichs, Ann. *The California Missions.* Minneapolis: Compass Point Books, 2002.

Isaacs, Sally Senzell. *Life in a California Mission.* Chicago: Heinemann Library, 2002.

Kennedy, Teresa. *California.* New York: Children's Press, 2001.

Keremitsis, Eileen. *Life in a California Mission.* San Diego: Lucent Books, 2003.

Staeger, Rob. *The Spanish Missions of California.* Broomall, PA: Mason Crest Publishers, 2003.

Weber, Valerie, and Dale Anderson. *The California Missions.* Milwaukee, WI: Gareth Stevens Pub., 2002.

# Organizations and Web Sites

### The California Mission Site

www.californiamissions.com

Read the history of each mission, see photos, and listen to music written by mission padres and Native Americans.

### California Missions

http://missions.bgmm.com

Learn more about each mission's history, architecture, and location.

### California Missions Resource Center

www.missionscalifornia.com

Take a "visual journey" through each mission, and see timelines, photos, and drawings of mission life.

# Places to Visit

### Mission San Juan Bautista

406 Second Street
San Juan Bautista, CA 95045
(831) 623-4528
www.oldmissionsjb.org
Step back in time and see what it was like to live at a mission.

### Mission San Juan Capistrano

26801 Ortega Highway
San Juan Capistrano, CA 92675
(949) 234-1300
www.missionsjc.com
See the oldest building in California and take a peek through the cat door.

# Important Words

**adobe** (uh-DOE-bee) – a building material made from sand, clay, water, and straw or manure that is dried in the sun and used to make bricks

**arcades** – arched, covered passageways

**baptized** – becoming a member of the church through a ceremony in which someone is either dipped in or sprinkled with water

**convert** – to cause to accept different beliefs

**cultures** – the languages, customs, ideas, and art of different groups

**droughts** (DROWTS) – periods of little rain

**facades** (fuh-SAHDZ) – the front of buildings

**looms** – machines for weaving cloth

**mass** – the celebration of the Eucharist in the Roman Catholic and some Protestant churches

**neophytes** (NEE-uh-fites) – newly baptized Native Americans at a mission

**padres** (PAH-drayz) – priests at a mission

**presidios** (prih-SEE-dee-ohz) – forts that the Spanish built for protection

**secularized** (SEK-yuh-luh-rized) – to take something, such as the missions, out of the church's control

# Index

Page numbers in **bold** indicate illustrations

# About the Author

Megan Gendell has written and edited children's books about outer space, spies, magic tricks, and dinosaurs. She is a former editor at Scholastic and a graduate of Columbia University. When she is not writing, she teaches and performs acrobatics in New York City. She sometimes studies at Circus Center in San Francisco and enjoys visiting the city's Mission Dolores.

**PHOTOGRAPHS** © 2010: age fotostock: 22 (Russ Bishop), 43 (Claver Carroll); akg-Images, London: 14; Alamy Images: 38 bottom right (Rodolfo Arpia), 38 top (Danita Delimont), 39 bottom left (Mike Dobel), 35 bottom (Julius Fekete), 29 (Michael Freeman), 26 (Thomas Hallstein), 35 top (Della Huff), 42 (NaturaLight), 9, 15 foreground, 38 bottom left (North Wind Picture Archives), 28 (Frank Vetere), 34 (Richard Wong); Bridgeman Art Library International Ltd., London/New York/California Historical Society Collections at the Autry: 12; Corbis Images: 5 top, 21 (Richard Cummins), 30 (Dave G. Houser), 8 (MAPS.com); Getty Images/ Jeff Hunter: 41; iStockphoto: 32 (Dana Baldwin), 34 map, 35 map (Sharon Day), cover, 40 (Eric Foltz), 15 background (Evgueni Groisman), 23 (Birgitte Magnus), 31 (Nancy Nehring), 6 (S. Greg Panosian), 39 bottom right (Ufuk Zivana), back cover, 3 (zts); MarkChurms.com: 24 (©2007), 20 (©2008); Courtesy of Mission San Juan Capistrano/www.missionsjc.com: 5 bottom, 25; Nativestock.com/Marilyn "Angel" Wynn: 36; Scholastic Library Publishing, Inc.: 44; ShutterStock, Inc./Elena Ray: 33; The Granger Collection, New York: 10, 13, 18; University of Southern California Library: 39 top (CHS-M17499), 19 (CHS-M19768), 4, 16 (CHS-M8002).